Mastering the Power of Hypnosis

How to use hypnosis to change lives

By John Cassidy-Rice

www.free-nlp.co.uk

Copyright and Legal Information

advice and, where appropriate, the advice of a suitably qualified professional should be sought. The author and publisher shall in no event be held liable to any party for any damages arising directly or indirectly from any use of this material. Any perceived slight of specific people or organizations is unintentional.

Every effort has been made to accurately represent this product and its potential and there is no guarantee that you will earn any money using these techniques and ideas. Any links to other websites are for information only and are not warranted for content, performance, accuracy or any other implied or explicit purpose.

About the Author

John Cassidy-Rice

John has been involved in NLP and Personal Development for over 15 years. A recognised and certified International Master NLP Trainer. He has become sought after as a Mentor in NLP. He is the co-founder and principle trainer of NLP Excellence running courses on a national and international basis (www.free-nlp.co.uk)

John has a relaxed refreshing humour and informative style. He is adept at using games, models and music to create an environment where learning is easy and fun. He has a reputation for getting results, a deep understanding of how the mind works and how language affects interaction in life.

His trainings are designed to dramatically increase the creativity, teamwork and performance of organisations and individuals through music and learning technologies. He has worked with many companies such as The Financial Times and Accenture. His work has taken him all over the United Kingdom, and also Internationally in Texas and Florida, USA, and Australia.

John is a Managing Partner for the Wizard of Ads, an international marketing company. This involves training, research and consultancy in marketing and advertising. A dynamic public speaker in this area.

Table of Contents

Introduction: The Power of Hypnosis

The field of hypnosis is widely misunderstood and this leads many people to miss out on the benefits it can bring.

For many the whole idea of hypnosis is tied up in comedy stage shows where people embarrass themselves by clucking like hens.

Or they have some vague idea of a man dangling a watch trying to get into the deeper recesses of their mind.

In fact the principles behind hypnosis have wide application in everyday life and people who learn the principles can have huge advantages.

> *"People who learn the principles of hypnosis can have huge advantages."*

Learning the principles of hypnosis can help you in many ways, including:

- Communicating more effectively with others
- Assisting other to overcome blocks and obstacles

- Achieving your goals and objectives more easily
- Improving your performance in sport or in business

In this book, we explain the truth about hypnosis and show how you can apply the principles in your life so that you can help yourself and help others.

To your success
John Cassidy-Rice

Section 1: Principles of Hypnosis
1.1: What Is Hypnosis?

It's useful to start by developing a clear understanding of what hypnosis is.

There is no agreed definition of hypnosis and you'll probably get a different answer to this depending on who you ask.

But equally, there are many common elements to these explanations that give a clear picture of what exactly is involved in hypnosis.

The popular impression of hypnosis links it very closely with sleep – not least because the word 'hypnosis' comes from the name of the Greek god for sleep. Many dictionaries also define hypnosis as a sleep-like state.

While hypnosis has some similarities with sleep it also has various characteristics that make it different.

> *"While hypnosis has some similarities with sleep it also has characteristics that make it different."*

Here are some of the characteristics of

hypnosis.

- **May be guided:** While states of hypnosis can occur naturally, the deepest and most useful hypnosis can result from being guided by another person. This process is known as induction. You can also guide yourself into this state through self-hypnosis. We'll look at the process of induction later.

- **Deep relaxation:** Hypnosis is a state of deep mental and physical relaxation and in that sense has similarities with sleep. However brain scans show that the brain remains alert during hypnosis.

- **Intensified focus and attention:** Hypnosis tends to involve strong focus and attention on one item or idea. This can apply particularly during the process of induction into hypnosis, where the hypnosis results from concentrating on one thing.

- **Distraction of the conscious mind:** The human mind can be split into two parts – the conscious mind, which focuses on what's important right now, and the unconscious mind, which stores all past memories and controls the emotions. One of the effects of hypnosis is to distract the conscious mind so that you can have more effective communication with the unconscious mind.

- **Heightened suggestibility**: During hypnosis the mind is more open to taking on board suggestions than it is during normal 'wakeful' states. This is the main reason why hypnosis is so powerful.

A key element of hypnosis is the concept of trance. We'll look at trance in more detail later but the general idea of trance is a very relaxed state of mind.

One of the clearest definitions of hypnosis is from the renowned hypnotherapist Milton Erickson, who we'll refer to later.

He said hypnosis is "A state of intensified attention and receptiveness to an idea or to a set of ideas."

While there are many other definitions, this is useful one to bear in mind as we go through the other steps in this book.

1.2: What Can Hypnosis Be Used For?

Now that we've introduced hypnosis, let's see how it can be used.

When you see how much you can do with hypnosis, you'll see how useful it is to learn. Here are some ways it can be used for yourself or others:

- **Controlling pain:** Anything from taking away a minor headache to dental or surgical techniques done without anaesthetic

- **Building confidence:** For example, you can use hypnosis to overcome feelings of shyness in social situations

- **Overcoming procrastination:** Remove blocks and obstacles that stop you taking action

- **Cut out unwanted habits:** Quit smoking and other unwanted habits such as nail biting

- **Lose weight:** Hypnosis can be used to help you lose weight by changing your behaviour and diet

- **Overcome stress and fear:** Hypnosis can help you get rid of fear and overcome feelings of stress and anxiety – either generally or in specific situations such as public speaking

- **Increase motivation**: you can use hypnosis to motivate yourself to achieve more and to reach bigger goals

- **Sleeping better**: Get rid of insomnia and get a good night's sleep for a change.

1.3: History of Hypnosis

The concepts behind hypnosis can be traced back thousands of years to ancient Egyptian papyrus scrolls and Sanskrit writing in India.

There is plenty evidence of 'trances' and 'sleeping temples' being used in healing.

However the modern concept of hypnosis is much more recent.

The development of hypnosis, as we know it today, can be traced back to the time when magnets were used to try and cure the body of disease. In the 16th century, a Swiss doctor named Paracelsus claimed to cure many patients by passing magnets over parts of their body.

The following a century an Irish faith healer named Valentine Greatrakes was touring England claiming to cure people just by laying on hands.

Mesmer's magnets
One of the most significant developments came after an Austrian doctor called Franz Anton Mesmer learned about the use of magnets in

medical treatment from a priest named Maximilian Hehl.

Mesmer took these magnets back to his practice in Vienna and began using them in treating patients.

There was a medical process common at the time which involved make a cut in the patient and then letting them bleed for a while – this was known as 'bloodletting'.

The magnet was then passed over the cut to stop the bleeding.

One day, while treating a patient, Mesmer could not find his magnets so passed a stick over the cut instead. The bleeding stopped.

This led Mesmer to claim that it was not the energy of the magnet that caused the bleeding to stop. He said it was magnetic energy coming from within the patient – which he called 'animal magnetism'.

> *Mesmer said the bleeding stopped not due to the magnet but because of "animal magnetism."*

Mesmer moved to France and became very popular and successful. This inevitably led to people becoming jealous and trying to criticise and discredit him and his methods.

He attempted to defend himself by asking the French king to set up a board of inquiry to support his claims. But this went badly wrong when the board came out against him.

As a result Mesmer had to leave France and although he continued to practice, he had lost his immediate influence.

Nevertheless others continued to practice 'mesmerism' although it remained controversial and unpopular with the medical establishment.

The birth of hypnosis
In the early 19th century, a young Scottish surgeon names James Braid attended a demonstration of mesmerism in London.

He was initially unimpressed and thought the whole thing was a fraud so he set out to discredit it.

However as he got more involved in studying it, he made some significant discoveries. What Braid noticed was that, although the mesmerist's hands were passing over the patient's body, the patient's eyes remained fixed in an upward stare.

Braid judged that the benefit of mesmerism did not come in the energy transfer but was due to the patient being in trance.

He coined a new term to describe the state that he noticed, which he called 'neuro-hypnosis'.

He described it in more detail in his 1840 book "Neurypnology", which was the first book on hypnosis as we know it today. Having coming up with the term hypnosis, Braid tried to change it to a description he felt was more appropriate but the name has stuck.

Braid judged the most important fact was that fixation on a single point or idea was what caused hypnosis to occur.

His discoveries also emphasized that the degree of hypnosis seemed to depend more on the subject than on the hypnotist.

Freud and psychoanalysis
By the late 19th century many others were taking an interest in the study and practice of hypnotism. One of those was the psychologist

Sigmund Freud who used it initially and then stopped.

There are various explanations given for his decision to stop using hypnosis but he went on to develop something he called 'talking therapy' which became psychoanalysis and became a very important aspect of psychology.

Some would argue that many of his techniques are simply hypnosis by another name.

Another important discovery in the development of hypnosis was in the early 20th century, when a French pharmacist named Emil Coué discovered 'autosuggestion' or what he called 'waking suggestion' – another important building block in hypnosis.

He discovered that the actual suggestion given by the hypnotist or therapist means nothing until it is accepted by the mind of the patient or client.

In short, his discovery was a very important point to understand in using hypnosis – all hypnosis is effectively self-hypnosis.

In other words, the subject is in control – the therapist simply guides the process.

Wider acceptance

There was a significant development in the understanding of hypnosis with publication in 1933 of the book "Hypnosis and Suggestibility" by Clark Hull. This was one of the first psychological studies of hypnosis.

During the war years, there was also some use of hypnosis in pain control and medical treatment – and by 1958, the American Medical Association approved the therapeutic use of hypnosis.

> **"All hypnosis is effectively self-hypnosis."**

Hypnosis was now in the mainstream and becoming increasingly popular and more widely-used.

The modern hypnotists

One of the biggest influences in hypnosis in the 20th century was the American therapist Milton Erickson.

He practiced hypnosis with clients every day for around 60 years and developed a view of hypnosis that has had a major influence on the development of the field.

The principle behind Erickson's view of hypnosis is that ambiguity causes trance. He uses vague suggestions rather than making specific requests and this led to him having great success.

> *"Erickson developed a view of hypnosis that has had a major influence on the development of the field."*

It's worth noting that there are other views of what makes successful hypnosis. George Estabrooks, for example, believed that hypnotic suggestions have to be direct and specific.

Both approaches have had success. So understanding hypnosis has to take account of the Erickson-style approach of being permissive/indirect and the other extreme of being authoritarian/direct.

Either approach – or some variation in between – may be appropriate depending on the circumstances or the client.

The key is to use your experience of hypnosis – combined with understanding the client's situation – to find the right one.

So, with that review of the history, let's look at how hypnosis can be used today.

1.4: Myths About Hypnosis

Before we go too far into explaining hypnosis, it's worth addressing some of the popular myths and misconceptions.

Believing many of these mistaken ideas prevents many people from harnessing the full potential of hypnosis to change their own lives and those of others.

Here are some of the most common misconceptions.

> *"As hypnosis requires concentration and focus, being intelligent may*

- **Intelligent people can't be hypnotised**
  There is some perception that people who can be hypnotised have low intelligence. There is no evidence to support this and actually the reverse is probably true.

  As being hypnotised requires a degree of concentration and focus, it is likely that being intelligent enables you to be hypnotised more easily.

- **I'll give away secrets**

People fear that under hypnosis they will say things they don't want to say. This impression is based on the idea that hypnosis happens because the hypnotist has power over his subject.

In fact the hypnotist is only the guide and you are in control of what you say. Clearly hypnosis can be used to help people relax and talk more easily or to remember things more clearly. But you are in control of deciding what you want to say.

- **I'll do something I don't want to do**
  This is one of the most common
  misconceptions about hypnosis and it
  arises partly by seeing people on stage
  clucking like hens.

  There are also stories and films about
  what people
  are alleged to
  have done
  under
  hypnosis.
  The fact is that
  the people who
  participate in
  stage shows do
  so with the full
  knowledge of
  what is going to happen.

  > **"People who participate in stage shows do so with the full knowledge of what is going to happen."**

  Your mind will prevent you from doing
  something which conflicts with your
  normal values and you may even break
  out from hypnosis if you strongly object
  to something being suggested.

- **I will feel under someone else's control**
  The process of hypnosis is often guided
  but is not controlled by the other person.

The subject remains in control and can decide to snap out of hypnosis at any moment if they truly feel the situation objectionable.

The hypnotist only has control to the degree that the subject allows them control at any moment.

- **I won't know what's happening**
Depending on how deep the trance, you may not be consciously aware of exactly what is happening.

  However you are unconsciously aware of what is happening and you can rely on your unconscious mind to keep you safe in the same way that it keeps you breathing and keeps your heart beating 24 hours a day.

- **I won't wake up**
The fear of not waking up arises partly from the belief that hypnosis is like sleep. Even people involved in hypnosis use terms like 'wakeful state' or 'waking up' that imply that connection.

  In truth, hypnosis is not the same as

sleep.

You can snap out of hypnosis as any second. In an emergency such as a fire, you would come out of hypnosis instantly. This may not be the case if you are sleeping.

- **I remember everything so I wasn't hypnotised**
  This is the opposite of fearing that you won't remember anything.

  People have this picture of hypnosis being such a deep state that they are unconvinced when they are able to follow everything that is happening.

  In fact a great deal of hypnosis happens in very light 'trance', which means you are aware of almost everything. We'll talk more about degrees of trance later.

So if these are the myths about hypnosis, let's go on to the truths and see how we can apply hypnosis to benefit our lives.

1.5: The Secret of Suggestion

The key to understanding how hypnosis works is knowing how the mind deals with suggestion.

The human mind is trained from an early age to respond to suggestions.

Our lives are shaped by the things other people say to us and the way we talk to ourselves.

If our parents and friends tell us something about ourselves, we often believe it even if it isn't true.

They tell us we're no good at sport so we don't take any interest in it.

> *"Suggestion is partly about what people say but it's also about how our imagination makes us respond to what people say."*

They tell us 'it will never work' so we don't try.

The thing is we get into the habit of believing these things so we don't take the trouble to find out if they are actually true.

The added power of imagination

Suggestion is therefore partly about what people say but it's also about how our imagination makes us respond to what people say.

For example, you try a sport for the first time and it doesn't go well. Maybe something happened during a game – perhaps you dropped a ball you were meant to catch. Somebody comments about that specific event.

In your mind, that comment becomes a suggestion that you are no good at this sport. At best it will affect your performance the next time. At worst it may mean you never try it again.

Different people react to this kind of suggestion in different ways – in part dependant on their degree of belief about themselves.

> *"We can use this power to train the mind with positive suggestions, rather than piling on more negative ones."*

Some people look for their own evidence of what is working and try to improve their performance. Others base their views largely on what others say – or even more damagingly what they believe others think.

The power of hypnosis is rooted in our response to suggestions.

The secret is that we can use this power to train the mind with positive suggestions, rather than piling on more negative ones.

The thing is that we are often dealing with years and years of negative suggestions and these cannot be overturned with one quick positive one.

In a sense, we need to teach the mind how to behave and respond positively.

Learned behaviour
This type of learned behaviour was first highlighted back in 1902 by an American doctor called William Twitmeyer.

He wrote an article in the Journal of the American Medical Association called the 'Knee Jerk Reflex'.

He observed that patients' knees would jerk when they were hit gently with a small hammer. But he noticed that when they became conditioned to this, the knees would begin to respond with a jerk when he simply told them he was going to hit them. He didn't even need to touch them.

This concept went unnoticed at the time but it was two years later – when a young Russian researcher called Ivan Pavlov detailed his experiences with dogs.

> **"The ability of individuals to learn or unlearn behaviour can vary."**

Pavlov had noticed that his dogs would naturally salivate when they could see he was about to feed them.

As part of an experiment, he sounded a bell or tuning fork at the same time as he was feeding them. Over time, they would link the ringing sound in their minds with food and become conditioned to salivate just at the sound of a ring even if he did not give them food.

This research became famous and the concept of conditioned behaviour and learned response became more widely recognised.

Unlearning behaviour
So, in a sense, one of the keys to hypnosis is

realizing that the mind can unlearn old thoughts and behaviours and replace them with new ones given the right conditions.

The ability of individuals to learn or unlearn behaviour can vary. Some people are more 'suggestible' than others.

Later, we'll look at some different tests you can use to show people how powerful suggestion is and to help them see how suggestible they are.

1.6: The Mind in Hypnosis

In this section, we'll look at what happens inside the mind during hypnosis.

One of the keys to understanding how the mind works is recognising the difference between the two separate parts of the mind – the Conscious Mind and the Unconscious Mind.

Of course the mind is not physically split in this way – this is simply a way of recognising that the mind has within it 'machinery' that serves different purposes.

In this case both are essential but we can work with the mind more effectively when we understand the significance of each.

Knowing the unconscious mind
Here are some of the characteristics of the unconscious mind:

- It is responsible for all the **bodily functions** that you're not thinking about all the time. It breathes you and beats your heart even when you are asleep. So you know you can trust it to look after you.

- It stores all your **memories**. Several scientific studies have shown that your brain contains memories of everything that has ever happened to you.

- It is the domain of the **emotions**. It's where you decide whether to feel happy or sad.

- It needs very **specific** instructions about what is required. You decide with your conscious mind what you want. You then trust the unconscious mind to get it for you.

- It maintains your instincts and generates your **habits**. It likes things to be the way that it's used to having them. In order for that to happen, repetition is required.

> "**What you say to yourself and to others needs to be positive and focused on the outcome you want.**"

- It is ambitious. It's **never satisfied**. It always wants something better for you.

- It's **symbolic** so reacts to symbols like

pictures or music, for example.

- It takes everything **personally**. It thinks anything it sees or hears relates to you. That's why it's so important that your thoughts and what you say to yourself and to others are positive and focused on the outcome you want. It's also important to surround yourself with positive people.

How the conscious mind is different
Here are some of the characteristics of the conscious mind.

- It is focused on the **current** moment. Your conscious mind is about awareness – the things you are thinking about right now.

- It is in touch with **reality**. The conscious mind deals with the information coming through all of your senses – what you can see, hear, feel, taste and smell.

- It processes **information**. The conscious mind deals with logic and facts.

- It makes **decisions**. After exploring the options, your conscious mind will make the decision.

- It gives **instructions**. Your conscious mind sets the direction for the unconscious mind.

Here are some examples of how that works in practice:

- If I ask you for your phone number, it comes into your conscious mind. A moment ago, it was in your unconscious mind.

- When you decide what to do, you use your unconscious mind. Your conscious mind will figure out the best way to make it happen.

- Your conscious mind will look at the facts of a situation. Your unconscious mind will determine your feelings about it.

The problem is that your conscious mind can get in the way when you are trying something new. It will come up with reasons something won't work or problems that will get in the way.

That's why you want to get the conscious mind out of the way when you want to change something about yourself – or someone else.

The secret of hypnosis is keeping the conscious mind busy or distracted while you make contact direct with the unconscious mind.

1.7: Understanding Trance

Trance is one of the building blocks of hypnosis so let's look at what trance is and how to recognise it.

The state you are when you are hypnotised is known as trance.

However many people are surprised to realise that trance is actually an everyday experience.

If you've ever been driving along a motorway and missed the junction you planned to use, you have been in a trance. It doesn't mean you weren't paying attention to the road ahead – but your mind was not focused on the fact that you needed to take that junction.

If you've ever been reading or watching television and then heard a partner saying they've been speaking to you but you've been ignoring them, that's another example of trance.

Essentially our mind is so focused on one thing that we don't notice others. That is trance and it's an everyday occurrence.

The difference between a hypnotic trance and

an everyday trance is that the hypnotic trance is deliberately created – usually with the help of another person. It is also likely to be deeper and longer-lasting than a 'driving' trance or a 'watching TV' trance.

Different levels of trance

There are a number of elements to look out for that will indicate to you that someone is in trance.

There are different levels of trance that will show in different ways.
For example:

Light trance

In a light trance, the subject will be feeling relaxed. They will be blinking more often or more slowly and they will be breathing more heavily. This is similar to the feeling just before falling asleep. People are used to this feeling and some will find it difficult to go beyond this level of relaxation initially.

When trance gets slightly deeper, the person will feel heavier and there may be 'catalepsy' or stiffness of some of the muscles. This could mean a hand staying up even if the person is very relaxed.

Medium trance

At deeper levels of trance, there can be more noticeable physical symptoms – smell or taste may change.

People can become more tolerant to pain and can be persuaded to have temporary amnesia – such as forgetting their name or certain numbers.

In the right conditions, most people can reach medium levels of trance.

Deep trance

At much deeper levels of trance, much greater physical control is possible – such as stiffening of the whole body – known as full body catalepsy.

People are much more tolerant of pain and can undergo surgical or dental treatments without anaesthetics.

They are also much more open to hypnotic suggestions. Not everyone can reach deeper levels of trance easily.

Section 1: Key Points

Characteristics of hypnosis
- May be guided
- Deep relaxation
- Intensified focus and attention
- Distraction of the conscious mind
- Heightened suggestibility

Possible Uses of hypnosis
- Controlling pain
- Building confidence
- Overcoming procrastination
- Cut out unwanted habits
- Lose weight
- Overcome stress and fear
- Increase motivation
- Sleep better

History of hypnosis
- Concepts can be traced back thousands of years.
- Hypnosis, as we know it today, can be traced back to the time when magnets were used to try and cure the body of disease in the 16th century.
- Austrian doctor called Franz Anton Mesmer began using them in treating

patients. He claimed it was not the energy of the magnet that caused the bleeding to stop but was 'animal magnetism'.

- Mesmer was discredited by French board of enquiry but others continued to practice 'mesmerism'.
- In the early 19th century, Scottish surgeon James Braid attended a demonstration of mesmerism in London and was initially unimpressed.
- However Braid said benefit was due to the patient being in trance. He coined a new term to describe the state that he noticed, which he called 'neuro-hypnosis'.
- In early 20th century, a French pharmacist named Emil Coué discovered 'autosuggestion'.
- During the war years, there was also some use of hypnosis in pain control and medical treatment – and by 1958, the American Medical Association approved the therapeutic use of hypnosis.

Popular Myths about hypnosis
- Intelligent people can't be hypnotised
- I'll give away secrets
- I'll do something I don't want to do
- I will feel under someone else's control

- I won't know what's happening
- I won't wake up
- I remember everything so I wasn't hypnotised

The power of suggestion
- The added power of imagination
- Learned behaviour
- Unlearning behaviour

Knowing the unconscious mind
- It is responsible for all the bodily functions
- It stores all your memories
- It is the domain of the emotions
- It needs very specific instructions about what is required
- It maintains your instincts and generates your habits
- It's never satisfied. It always wants something better for you.
- It reacts to symbols
- It takes everything personally

How the conscious mind is different
- It is focused on the current moment
- It is in touch with reality
- It processes information
- It makes decisions

- It gives instructions

Different levels of trance
- Light
- Medium
- Deep

Section 2: Hypnosis in Practice
2.1: The Hypnosis Interview

Now that we've looked at what hypnosis is, we'll go on to discuss how you can use it to help other people to change their results.

Hypnosis is a very powerful technique that allows you to help people make big changes in their lives. It's a skill that should therefore be used with great integrity and care.

> *"Hypnosis is a very powerful technique that allows you to help people make big changes in their lives."*

You should only use it in situations where you have fully explained to your client what is going to happen and you have their full permission to follow the process.

You should only follow this type of questioning in an environment which is confidential and in which you are both comfortable.

Finding out what they want
The first stage in that process is talking to the other person – your client – and finding out

what they want to change.

You need to use this conversation to find out exactly what the problem is and then collect information about the key events that have happened in their life that have led up to this situation.

You are going through these steps in 'normal' mode and not even discussing hypnosis until later in the process. This is purely information gathering.

Below we've suggested some questions you might use as part of this process.

Before you ask these questions, it's important to spend some time on less sensitive issues to get to know them better. This will help you build up a rapport that makes it easier for them to share their story with you.

As you follow the answers to the questions, remember to be looking out for what they don't say and keep track of their non-verbal communication to get a clear idea of what they are really thinking.

Look out for any suggestion that the person is blaming someone else for the issue rather than taking responsibility for it. For example, when someone says something like "My partner says I should..." they are not yet fully invested in the process and won't be ready to make the necessary change.

Here are some questions you can use to help find out as much as possible. Note that the questions relate to solving a problem – you can change the wording slightly if the focus is more positive such as goal achievement.

- **Why are you here today?**
  Note the soft question – your not asking them about the problem. Make sure you go through all the reasons they have come to see you; they will probably not tell you the real reason right away. Keep saying "What else?" until you are satisfied you have got the real issue.

- **How do you know you have this problem?**
  Here you are looking to find out exactly what they do and what goes through their mind when they are having the problem.

- **If this problem was to disappear for good, how would you know it has gone?**
  Get them to imagine life without the problem

Be especially careful with the notes you take in response to these questions. Write down their exact words because you will be able to use these words when you design your solution.

- **How long have you had this problem?**

- **Was there ever a time when you didn't have this problem?**

- **What do you believe about this problem?**

- **What happened the first time you had this problem?**

- **What has happened since then?**

- **Tell me about your family – parents, brothers and sisters – in relation to this problem**
  Get them to describe specifically how each person relates to the problem. The

connections may not be immediately obvious but they could be important.

- **Tell me about your childhood in relation to this problem.**

- **What is it that you don't have to do because you have this problem?**
  This and the next question are designed to find out if there is 'secondary gain' i.e. some benefit in not solving the problem.

- **What would you have to stop doing if this problem disappeared?**

If necessary, explain to client that they have a conscious and an unconscious mind.

"You use the information in this process to help people create solutions to their problems."

Explain that they should trust the first thing that comes to their mind – even if it seems odd – as this is likely to be the unconscious response.

- **Ask your unconscious mind when your decided to create this problem**

- **Ask your unconscious mind if there is a purpose for having this problem**

- **Ask your unconscious mind if there is something you need to learn or pay attention to that would make this problem disappear**

- **Ask your unconscious mind if it is willing to support us in getting rid of this problem today.**

Using these questions, you should be able to build a picture of exactly what the problem is and you should also have a good idea of possible causes.

You'll use the information you have gathered in this process to create a solution for them.

Case Study: Fear of Public Speaking

Joe was 25 and one of the company's top salespeople earning close to six figures a year.

He was being marked down for great things in the company but one thing was holding back his progress to the next level.

Joe was one of the best in one-to-one situations with individual clients.

But he'd freeze with terror when asked to speak to a large group.

Progressing to the next level meant he'd need speak to groups of clients and make formal presentations. To really make his mark in the company, he'd also need to go on stage at sales conferences.

Through hypnosis he worked on getting rid of his fear and building positive anchors into the process of preparing for and giving presentations.

Even after just one session, Joe saw a huge difference because he immediately said 'yes' when invited to give a presentation. After a couple more sessions, he was brimming with confidence and starting to look forward to the next one.

Now he's lined up to give a keynote presentation at the next sales conference on how he landed a £3 million order.

Part of that will be a rerun of the presentation he gave to the client's global board to seal the deal.

2.2: Preparing the Client for Hypnosis

The next step in the process is to let the client know what to expect during hypnosis.

This is especially important if it is a first time for them. You should never rush someone into hypnosis without their agreement and without them understanding what is going to happen.

So let's cover the points you need to go over with a client before you start doing any hypnosis.

Explaining the background
If the client has no previous experience of hypnosis, you will probably need to address some misconceptions.

You'll find many of the points that we covered in the first section of this book are helpful background for clients.

It's useful to explain a bit about the history of hypnosis and about the range of ways in which it can help people.

There are a few specific points you should cover:

- **Deal with any misconceptions**
  You will find that many clients come with pre-conceived ideas about hypnosis. These may be wildly inaccurate based on stage shows or TV programmes.

  Take time to find out if they have any misconceptions and make sure you address them by dealing with any questions they have.

  In the first section, we covered many of the popular misconceptions and you may find it useful to go through these with clients.

- **Tell them they shouldn't expect to feel hypnotised**

  > *"Explain to them that trance is a normal state which is just like feeling very relaxed."*

  Many people have an idea of what they expect to feel like when they are hypnotised.

  Explain to them that trance is a normal state which is just like feeling very relaxed. This will not only address concerns they may have, it also pre-

suggests relaxation to them.

You can point out to them times they have been in a trance in their everyday life – such as the examples when driving a car or watching television that we covered in the first section.

- **Assure them they remain in control**
  One of the biggest concerns for many people is that they somehow become under the control of the hypnotist.

  Make sure your clients understand that the hypnosis depends on them and that they are in control – that all hypnosis is self-hypnosis.

  Reassure them they will only accept suggestions under hypnosis that are consistent with their normal values and beliefs.

These explanations are an important part of building trust and confidence with the client. This step will help determine the success of the later stages.

2.3: Suggestibility Tests

When the client is beginning to look forward to hypnosis, it's a great time to introduce some suggestibility tests.

These have the benefit of addressing many of the misconceptions about hypnosis. But they also get the client used to the idea of trance and help them recognise how normal and easy it is to achieve.

The suggestibility tests will help the client convince themselves that they are suggestible.

So point out to them that this is a good thing:

- Tell them that it's good to have the ability to communicate with your unconscious mind

- Explain that being suggestible means you can give messages to your body that will benefit you

Here are three suggestibility tests you can easily use with a client:

- Dictionary and balloon test

- Finger vice test

- Postural sway test

These tests are fun but also very powerful in helping the client to go into trance.

Let's look at how to use each of them.

Dictionary and balloon test
Make sure you are in a space where both you and the client have a little room to move around. Then say to the client:

> *Please stretch both of your hands out in front of you at about shoulder height, with your palms facing down*

> *Close your eyes*

> *Now turn your right hand over so that this palm is facing up*

> *I'd like you to imagine a heavy book in that hand – a large dictionary. Imagine it's so heavy that's it's starting to push your right hand down, down, DOWN*

*Now imagine a large yellow balloon tied to
your left wrist*

*It's filled with helium and it's very light – so
light that your left hand is now lifting, lifting,
LIFTING*

*Imagine that book in your right hand getting
heavier and heavier pushing your hand
down*

*While that balloon is getting lighter all the
time and pulling your left hand up*

Continue these suggestions as necessary
until you see a noticeable difference in the
position of the two hands

Then ask the client to open their eyes

If there is a noticeable difference in the
hands – which there usually is – tell the
client this means they are very suggestible
and that their unconscious mind will be
open to change and to positive suggestion

Finger vice test
Say to the client:

Clasp your hands together in front of you

with the fingers interlocked

Lift your two forefingers so that they are pointing upward

Move your fingers so that they are about an inch apart and freeze them in that position

Clasp your other fingers very tightly together

Now imagine a small clamp round your two forefingers

I'm now going to turn the screw on that clamp and I want you to notice what happens (make the motion of turning the clamp)

Look how the fingers are moving closer together

Continue this process until the two fingers are noticeably much closer together

Again when the fingers have moved together, tell the client that means they are very suggestible and that their unconscious mind will be open to change and to positive suggestion

Postural sway test

Make sure you are in a space where both you and the client have a little room to move around. Then say to the client:

> *Close your eyes and look up towards the ceiling with your eyes closed*
>
> *Now imagine that you are swaying backward and forwards – safely of course*
>
> *You are falling, falling, falling...*
>
> *I will catch you*
>
> *Now come back and open your eyes*

Most clients get a sensation of falling but realise they are not actually falling. Point out that this shows how suggestible they are and that their unconscious mind will be open to change and to positive suggestion

These tests will help clients who are unfamiliar with hypnosis realise that it is a natural state.

> *"These tests will help clients who are unfamiliar with hypnosis realise that it is a natural state."*

In fact some of them may be surprised that it feels so normal.

You may find it useful to do more than one of the tests as some work better than others for different people.

Very occasionally none of the tests work. If this happens, simply point out to the client that it doesn't mean they are not hypnotised and it can reassure them they remain in control.

It's usually best not to imply that the level of change they see on those tests is a predictor of how deeply they will go into hypnosis. This could lead them to go less deeply than they might otherwise.

It will pre-suggest to them that they should go into trance easily and it will make them more comfortable and excited about moving forward to the next stage.

Case Study: Stress Headaches

Sue was 34 and a busy GP in a hectic city centre practice.

Almost every day, she'd find that she had a bad headache when she'd completed her afternoon surgery.

Of course she had easy access to pain killers that would take the problem away. But she realised that this was not a long-term solution.

She loved her job but was just struggling to cope with the pace of the demands on her day.

After just one hypnosis session, she noticed a big difference in her ability to manage the stress.

Over two or three sessions, she learned to work on releasing muscle tension rather than letting it build up.

She also learned some self hypnosis techniques that she could use on a daily basis to increase her relaxation.

Now she's thrown the painkillers away.

She's also started recommending hypnosis to many of her clients as a way to address the root of the problem rather than just the symptoms.

2.4: The Pendulum Effect

There are various ways of communicating directly with the unconscious mind without going into a full trance.

One of the best known of these is using a pendulum to get answers directly from the unconscious mind.

Why would you use a pendulum?
A pendulum is useful in situations where it is not possible to go into a deep trance.

This could occur because there is not enough time or because it's not a good location.

Sometimes the client is not ready to go into trance or is not able to get relaxed enough.

A pendulum can also be used as a convincer to show people the benefits of direct communication with the unconscious mind.

How to use a pendulum
First, you need something you can use as a

pendulum – a long string or chain with a weight at the end. Ideally you want to use a pendulum that comes with a clip that allows it to hang from an outstretched finger. These are available quite cheaply online and from 'New Age' shops.

The best way to use the pendulum is to have the client rest their elbow on a table with the forearm almost vertical. The hand should be totally relaxed so that it is dangling in mid-air.

When the hand is dangling in that position, you have arm catalepsy which is an indication of some degree of trance.

You should then have them hold the pendulum lightly between the thumb and forefinger or attach the clip to their forefinger so that the pendulum dangles lightly from their hand.

You are going to ask questions that usually have a yes/no answer so you will need to ask the client's unconscious mind to identify these signals.

So when you have the client with the pendulum hanging, tell them to ask their unconscious mind to give a clear signal for 'yes'. Then ask it to give a different signal for 'no'.

Sometimes it helps to give a demonstration of possible responses. Move the pendulum from left to right and say 'sometimes unconscious minds like to give a signal for yes that looks like this'. Then move the pendulum so that it swings from front to back and say 'sometimes unconscious minds like to give a signal for yes that looks like this'.

Then ask the unconscious mind to give its signals.

If the signals are not clear enough, ask the unconscious mind to make the signals clearer.

Some people like to draw up a pendulum chart to place under the pendulum indicating the position of 'yes' and 'no' plus possibly other answers such as 'don't know' or 'maybe'.

When to use a pendulum
You should use a question to get answers to questions which normally have a 'yes' or 'no' response'

Some typical questions might be:

- Do you know when I created this problem?

- Are you willing to let this problem go?
- Are you ready to start working on it now?
- Will this problem be resolved within the next 24 hours?
- Is there another problem?

How does the pendulum work?
The pendulum works because it amplifies tiny muscle movements in your arm through what is known as an 'ideomotor' response.

Sometimes the client is hesitant about believing the pendulum responses. It's important to tell them that they should trust these responses from their unconscious mind.

Sometimes it's a good idea to block their view of the pendulum so that they don't feel they are influencing the result by watching it.

Other ideomotor signals
It's not essential to have a pendulum to make use of 'ideomotor' responses. You could simply ask the client to rest one hand on their knee with the fingers hanging loose – without touching the knee.

You then ask the unconscious mind to allocate one finger as 'yes' and another as 'no'. A slight movement of the finger would indicate the response for that finger.

Or you could use four fingers and make them A, B, C and D to give you more options.

Case Study: Exam Nerves

Brian was 24 and studying to be an accountant while working full-time in a large company.

He'd recently failed his professional exams for the second time and was considering giving up the process.

He was frustrated because he was doing well at work and he knew he had the necessary knowledge. He just went into panic when it came time for the exam.

He was puzzled because he's done really well at school and university. But it seemed a whole different ball game when he had to work all day and his career was at stake.

He decided to give it one more chance. His boss was supportive because he valued his work and advised him to try and find some way of dealing with the exam nerves. So Brian decided to give hypnosis a go.

A series of hypnosis sessions helped him deal with the anxiety and helped him improve his memory and concentration when studying. Alongside this, he made some changes to his studying routine to make it fit more easily around his work schedule.

Next time round, he passed the exam with a merit award and is now making great progress in his career. He also reports that he remembers a lot more detail when in client meetings and he's able to make a much bigger contribution.

2.5: The Principles of Induction

When you have completed the client interview and the suggestibility tests, the client should be ready to go into trance.

So the next stage in the process is where you guide them into trance – this is known as 'induction'.

In this chapter, we'll look at the key steps you need to include in the induction process. In the following chapter we'll look at an outline script for the induction process.

The keys to a successful induction
There are a number of points to bear in mind as you lead the client into trance.

- **Understanding and purpose**
  Successful trance depends on the client having a high degree of comfort about what is going to happen during the process. So you should make sure you have answered any questions in advance.

  You should also take care to ensure that you are both agreed on the outcomes you want to achieve from the session.

- **Comfortable position**
  Make sure the client is in a comfortable position. You should have chosen an environment that is as private, quiet and comfortable as possible.

  Encourage them to lie back or stretch out so that they feel naturally relaxed.

- **Hypnotic voice**
  You've probably heard people using the term 'hypnotic voice' to describe someone with a naturally deep or slow voice. Well it's true there probably are some voices that are naturally more effective at leading people into trance.

  > *"What matters is not what your voice is like naturally but how you use it to maximize the hypnotic effect."*

  But equally there are many successful hypnotists whose voices don't fit into this category. What matters is not what your voice is like naturally but how you use it to maximize the hypnotic effect.

First your voice must convey confidence. If there is any hesitation in your speech, this will be conveyed to the patient and will make them uncomfortable.

Naturally your voice must also encourage relaxation. It should be soft and slow – almost monotonous like a tap dripping – to encourage the patient to fall into trance.

When your words are encouraging the patient to relax and go into trance, the tome of your voice should do the same thing.

You could even yawn during the induction to encourage the patient to do the same.

You can encourage the process by emphasizing certain words – for example, 'you are feeling sooooo relaaaaxed'.

Although you may be speaking quietly make sure it's not so quiet that the patient can't hear what you are saying.

- **Utilisation**
  During the induction – and indeed at later stages during hypnosis – you can incorporate what is happening around into your words.

  For example, if a telephone rings in the background, you can incorporate it by saying 'as you listen to that ringing sound, you feel more and more relaxed.'

  You can also make reference to what they are doing: 'I'm not sure if you've noticed that your breathing is slowing down.'

  Or you could say: 'In a moment you're going to blink...'. Of course they're going to blink anyway but unconsciously they feel they have responded to your command – especially if you say something like 'That's right!' when they do blink.

  This type of utilization acts as great convincer to assure the client that the process is 'working'.

  Milton Erickson was a master of noticing the small things and he believed greatly in letting the hypnosis process flow according to where the client was at any moment.

- **Embedded commands and suggestions**
  The principle of embedded commands and suggestions applies at all stages during the hypnosis process.

  It works by placing emphasis on certain words in a sentence so that they are communicated as a command or suggestion.

  For example: 'I'm not sure if you've noticed that you are ready to *go deeper into trance.*'

  By putting emphasis on the words 'deeper into trance' you are telling them to go deeper into trance and

  > **"You need to keep deepening the hypnosis until the relaxation is mental as well as physical."**

  they will follow this as an instruction – even though the question is not phrased as one.

- **Deepening**
  When the client is going into trance, you can use a number of techniques to encourage them to make that trance deeper.

  When they have started going into trance they will respond more easily to these suggestions.

  In the previous section, we looked at the indications for different depth levels of hypnosis.

  However, you'll find that it's normally not necessary to reach the very deep levels when you're working with a client on straightforward issues.

  What you'll find is that in light hypnosis, the relaxation is mainly physical.

  You need to keep deepening the hypnosis so that the relaxation is also mental so that they will be more open to your therapeutic suggestions.

It's therefore important to be able to recognise the difference between relaxation that is only physical and relaxation that is also mental.

- **Recognising trance**
  Naturally, one of the most important steps in the induction process is being able to recognise when the client has reached the level of trance you are looking for.

  Here are the indications you should look out for to confirm that the client has reached a degree of relaxation that is mental as well as physical.

  - o Flaccid facial muscles
  - o Deep, relaxed breathing
  - o Fluttering eyelids
  - o Completely relaxed appearance
  - o Slight smile on face

You should continue the process of deepening relaxation until you

"At this point you know the client is hypnotised and they know it too."

notice most of these signs. Some clients will reach it very quickly, while others will take a little longer.

You could carry out a small test by picking up the client's hand at the wrist and lifting it a few inches before letting it gently fall in to their lap.

It should drop with no resistance. You should tell them you are going to do this and this will help act as a convincer.

At this point you know the client is hypnotised and they know it too – even though they may later say they didn't feel hypnotised.

- **Awareness of client**
  While hypnosis is generally a safe and comfortable process, you need to take responsibility for the welfare of your client while they are in your care.

  Very occasionally you may have a client who reacts very strongly under hypnosis – for example by crying a lot or exhibiting very strong emotional reactions.

  In most situations, it is best not to

pursue this emotion with the client. It is better to first take them in their trance to a place where they feel comfortable and relaxed and then take them out of trance.

Have a discussion with them out of trance before you decide how to proceed.

So now that we have covered the principles of induction, let's look at the steps for carrying out an actual induction.

Case Study: Nail Biting

Jane was a 21-year old student who'd had a problem with nail-biting since she was in primary school.

She'd got used to it and didn't even mind when her friends ribbed her about it. Truth is she wasn't even aware of it herself when she did it. It was only when others mentioned it to her or she looked at her untidy nails.

But as she got closer to planning the next stage of her career, she realised that it might become a problem.

A friend told her about the power of hypnosis and she went to find out whether it could help.

After just one session, she began to feel a lot more confident and found herself much more aware of the problem.

This awareness of the problem helped her recognise more about what was causing it and she was able to feed this back to the hypnotherapist in further sessions.

After a couple of follow-up sessions, the nail-biting habit disappeared completely and she discovered new levels of self esteem and confidence.

She's now looking forward to starting her career soon. She'll be working in a large office and she doesn't believe that she would have been happy there if she'd still been biting her nails all the time.

2.6: The Induction Process

There are many different techniques for taking the client into trance.

We'll look here at one simple approach that should work in most situations.

We've included some other examples in the scripts section. You'll also find many free scripts available on the internet and in other hypnosis books.

You'll also find you can easily vary this script to suit your own style and to utilize the circumstances in the moment.

Relaxation induction

As you sit there, I want you to relax your whole body and take a deep breath.

Let the breath out very slowly, relaxing your whole body.

Now just close your eyes and listen to my voice.

I want you now to focus on an imaginary spot in the middle of your forehead. As you focus on that spot, you will feel the relaxation spread through your entire body.

The relaxation starts with the muscles in your scalp and works down through all the muscles in your head – your forehead and all your facial muscles.

It spreads through your neck and your chest and your back all the way to your waist.

It continues over your hips and your thighs all the way down your legs and your feet.

Your entire body is becoming more and more relaxed.

As you listen to my voice, you will notice that your arms are becoming tired and heavy. Your legs feel heavier and more tired. Your head and your neck are feeling tired and heavy.

Your whole body is feeling heavy and tired. As I continue talking, your arms and your legs – all the parts of your body – are becoming

"You can vary this script to suit your own style and utilize the circumstances in the moment."

83

more and more tired. They feel loose, limp and relaxed.

As you listen to my voice, you are drifting off into feeling very restful, calm and peaceful.

Your mind is now drifting as if it was on a cloud, so relaxed.

Your body continues to feel more and more tired, your limbs are heavier as you go deeper and more deeply relax.

You are now enjoying deep, warm, restful, peaceful, dreamless sleep... the most wonderful sleep you have ever known.

Your eyes are getting heavier and heavier... they are closed even more tightly now.

You are feeling so relaxed now... all muscle tension has disappeared

Any mental tension has gone completely... everyday concerns seem so far away

"So now that we have the client relaxed in hypnosis, what are we going to do?"

Every word I say makes you feel more and more

relaxed, more, deeper and deeper into sleep

Until I give you the signal to waken up, only sleep and relaxation seems to matter

You would continue deepening with this script until you have reached the level of relaxation you want.

You could develop it by adding in convincers such as suggesting they have a light helium balloon tied to one of their fingers and that this is lifting their finger.

So now that we have the client relaxed in hypnosis, what are we going to do?

They'll be feeling great at that moment and will quite happily sit there in that way.

But you are there for a purpose so let's look at how we can best make use of this trance.

Case Study: Fear of Dentist

Frank was a highly successful 34 year old lawyer who was hoping to be made partner in his firm.

He knew as a partner he'd have to spend a lot more time in court, where appearances matter a great deal. His problem was that he had serious problems with his teeth and this was very noticeable to others.

He'd put off going to the dentist for years because he was just terrified of the dentist chair.

Years of missing out on necessary treatment had now led to serious problems.

Nobody in the firm had ever made any comment but he feared that his appearance might count against him so he decided he had to face up to his fear.

A series of hypnosis sessions covered a number of issues such as dealing with anxiety to management of pain and in less than a month he was able to make an appointment to see the dentist. Previously he couldn't even face the idea of making an appointment.

He explained his past fear to the dentist who went out of her way to make him comfortable.

In fact, he felt fine when he went for his first appointment. As he expected, he need a series of follow up visits to put right the years of neglect but he'll soon have the best smile in the firm – especially when they make him a partner!

2.7: Designing Therapy

Now that you have the client in trance, it's time to use the opportunity to make positive changes in their life.

So let's have a look at how you can influence them positively.

This is the section when you get to talk directly to their unconscious mind and to get over the message of change that you have decided upon.

The exact words you use will depend on what you want them to change.

"The unconscious mind takes everything literally so choose your words very carefully."

We've included some sample scripts in the appendix for different types of issues.

In developing your scripts, you should go back to what they said during the initial interview.

Play back to them some of the things they said about how there life would be better if they made this change.

For example if they talked about how increased confidence would improve their relationships, you should say: 'your greater confidence means you are now meeting lots of interesting and attractive people and means you are now enjoying great relationships just as you always wanted.'

Just remember in this process that the unconscious mind takes everything literally so choose your words very carefully, keep your language positive and stay focused on the outcome you want.

Using stories and symbols
Take into account some of the other keys to the unconscious mind that we discussed in the previous section and use them in this part. So include some stories and symbols that help to get your message across.

You use these symbols to colour your language. For example:

- Rather than say 'your fear is going away', you could say: 'your fear is drifting away like a small white cloud on a windy day. One minute it was there and now it has gone completely.'

- Rather than say 'you are reaching your goals', you say: 'watch as that flock of birds flies high in the sky racing towards its destination in the same way that you are heading quickly towards achieving what you have always wanted.'

- Rather than say 'you are becoming more confident', say: 'like a flower blossoms in springtime, you are developing new confidence and belief in yourself that will transform you into a new person.'

When the client is in trance you have a great opportunity to pile on lots of positive information.

Take every opportunity to give them many positive messages relative to the issue you are focusing on.

While it's sometimes useful to follow a script, it's often a good idea to use this as a guide to make sure you cover everything.

It can work well to allow your own unconscious mind the flexibility to come up with ideas for the right thing to say.

Post-hypnotic suggestions

In many cases, an important part of the talk you give when they are in trance is a message about how they should behave after they come out of trance.

The post-hypnotic suggestion is something that you say during the trance but which they respond to after.

- It may be **immediate**: 'When you awake you will feel energised.'

- It may be at a **specific date** in the future: 'Next time you are on a stage getting ready to speak, you will feel full of confidence.'

- It may be at **specific events** each time they occur: 'Every time you feel the desire for a cigarette, you will immediately reach for a mint instead.'

> **"The right type of post-hypnotic suggestion can last for weeks, months or even years."**

A good post-hypnotic suggestion is closely tied with what the person wants – otherwise they will not be motivated to follow it up.

But the right type of post-hypnotic suggestion can last for weeks, months or even years.

The reality is that it probably only needs to work a few times because it will by then have created the new behaviours as normal.

Coming out of trance

When you have covered the full message that you want to get across, it's time to bring the client out of trance. This is one of the easiest parts of the process.

You can do this by saying 'In a moment I'm going to count from 1 to 5 and on each count I want you to gradually awaken so that by number 5 you are fully alert and energized ready to move ahead as the new you.'

On each number, you can make a positive suggestion: '1 – starting to awaken, 2 – beginning to feel more alert, 3 – gradually stretching and feeling fresh, 4 – feeling great and ready to act on your positive experiences her today and coming fully awake as I count 5.'

You may need to allow the client a few moments to collect their thoughts and waken up as they open their eyes.

Case Study: Driving Anxiety

Barry was a 52-year old finance director who'd worked for 24 years in the company head office in Central London.

He'd travel to work on the train every day and lived a short walk from the railway station. He said he loved walking and walked everywhere.

So he'd never had to face up to his driving anxiety. Many people don't like driving but a surprisingly large number have severe anxiety if they have to drive.

It is not only frightening but can be dangerous.

However it became a real issue when the company decided to relocate to an office in the country. For Barry, the only way to get there was drive.

He was close to his planned retirement and there was no way he wanted to give up the job now. So he had to deal with the issue.

Hypnosis helped him understand why he had the problem and allowed him to work on the anxiety.

After just two sessions, he was travelling comfortably in cars as a passenger. The following month, he hired a car and took his wife for a weekend away.

Now he's not only looking forward to the new job, he's discovered a new interest in visiting the churches in small villages he'd never been to before.

2.8: Outcomes and Evaluation

As with any type of work with clients, the work is never completed until they have the outcome they want.

That's why it's important that you continue to work with them to monitor progress.

If they have not got the results, you need to work with them to identify why not.

It may be that they still have an issue causing a block that needs to be dealt with first.

> *"If the client is happy with the outcome they may suggest other issues they want to address."*

Sometimes, you'll find you've addressed the issue but it has highlighted something else that needs to be worked on.

Indeed if the client is happy with the outcome they may suggest to you other things they want to address.

Sometimes the issue is that they don't really want to solve the problem. In this case hypnosis will not work. If this seems to be a problem, one way to get round it is to give them a 'task' that will prove that they are willing to act.

Tasks could include writing out a cheque to a cause they don't like which will be sent if they don't follow through. Or it could involve making a call to someone with whom they have a problem.

There are many cases where carrying out such a task has solved the problem by itself.
This stage is important not only for the client in helping make sure they get the outcome.

But for you as a therapist, it's important always to know what works and what doesn't. Of course, you can never guarantee that what applies to one person will apply in the same way to another.

As in any field of expertise, constant practice will lead you towards even better results.

2.9: Taking Care with Hypnosis

As hypnosis has very powerful potential, it's important that you use your knowledge with care and integrity.

There are several steps you can take to make sure you use your expertise to get the best results possible for you and your clients without taking any risks.

Here are a few steps you should bear in mind:

- **Don't over-claim or over-promise**
  While it's important to make people aware of the great results that are possible with hypnosis, you need to make clear that results will depend on them as much as you.

  For example, people need to be willing to change their behaviour to get results.

  If you claim that they will get results and they do not make these changes, they will end up being disappointed and will accuse you of misleading them.

- **Stick to your field of competence**

It's usually a good idea to limit your work to areas such as stress reduction, habit control (such as weight loss or giving up smoking) and performance improvement unless you have specific skills and training to go into more complex psychological issues.

If clients have a need for more specific psychological or psychiatric treatment, they should consult a suitably qualified professional.

- **Avoid clients with traumatic issues**
  People who clearly have highly repressed or traumatic issues may need special support and guidance.

  If it becomes clear to you that someone has such issues, you may need to take them out of hypnosis and refer them to someone with suitable expertise.

- **Be careful when dealing with medical issues**
  Always ensure that a client has consulted a medical doctor about any symptoms that give cause for concern.

  For example, recurring headaches may

be a sign that they need to learn to relax but it may be a warning of something more serious.

Similarly hypnosis can help deal with the symptoms of some medical problems but it should not be presented as a substitute for proper medical care.

Never claim to be able to cure any type of medical problem through hypnosis.

- **Consider recording sessions**
  Unless you know a client well, you may need to consider protecting yourself against unjustified accusations by recording the session (with their agreement.)

  When you are dealing with a client of the opposite sex, you may want to consider having another witness present or nearby.

If you use common sense and don't attempt to present hypnosis as a miracle cure, you should be on safe ground.

2.10: Self Hypnosis

One of the most powerful secrets of hypnosis is that you can learn to use in on yourself as well as others.

This means you can use self-hypnosis to change your own results and behaviour. But it also means you can teach clients how to use it to build on the results they get working with you.

All hypnosis is self hypnosis
As we learned in the history of hypnosis, Emil Coué argued that all hypnosis is self-hypnosis as the person who makes the change is the client not the therapist.

His discovery of the power of autosuggestion emphasised that the way we think all the time determines how we feel and what we do.

In fact, people with problems and negative beliefs have actually been hypnotising themselves for years to develop the beliefs that lead to the problems.

Someone who constantly tells themselves they can't do something ends up believing it.

In many cases this develops into a phobia or anxiety around the issue that makes the problem even worse.

Self hypnosis is simply a way to increase the chances of changing our thinking from negative to positive.

The only major difference between self hypnosis and guided hypnosis is that, with guided hypnosis, someone else tells you what to do.

There are some advantages in this in that another person can more easily judge whether you are deeply enough in trance, for example.

And many people find they go deeper into trance working with a hypnotherapist.

Some also feel better about having someone else give them instructions and positive comments. They believed the negative comments from others over many years so they need to hear the positive ones from someone else too.

At the same time, learning self-hypnosis is a very powerful skill. You can use it at any time and in any situation to improve your results.

Talking yourself into trance

Once you have learned the techniques, you can go into self-hypnosis even for a few seconds to deal with challenging situations.

The key to self-hypnosis is being able to take yourself through the induction process.

Once you have passed the induction process, the way you make suggestions is much the same as when working with a guide.

The key to learning self-induction is maintaining the ability to concentrate on the induction as you go through the steps.

You need to learn to relax yourself physically and mentally while still remaining focused on giving yourself instructions.

Case Study: Sleep problems

Jill was a 28 year old high-flyer who'd just been made HR director.

She was doing really well in the office but the workload and stress were taking their toll and she was not getting a proper night's sleep when she got home.

She'd had a similar problem as a student but then it seemed a normal part of the student lifestyle and she'd not bothered too much about it.

Now she could not take a nap in the afternoon to catch up. And she had to be on the ball all the time to justify the firm's faith in promoting her at such a young age.

Her busy work schedule did not leave her much time for appointments so she decided to learn self-hypnosis to help herself relax at the end of the day and to prepare for a great night's sleep.

It took her a few days to learn the process of teaching herself to relax but once she had mastered it, she was able to build it easily into her daily routine.

Now she uses the process to unwind just before she sleeps and to plant positive suggestions about relaxing and having a great night's sleep.

She's amazed to discover that the quality of her sleep means she actually needs less sleep than before. And she's also learned to use that self-hypnosis technique just after lunch to give herself extra energy for the afternoon.

Section 2: Key Points

The Hypnosis Interview
- Finding out what they want

Preparing the Client for Hypnosis
- Deal with any misconceptions
- Tell them they shouldn't expect to feel hypnotised
- Assure them they remain in control

Suggestibility Tests
- Dictionary and balloon test
- Finger vice test
- Postural sway test

The Pendulum Effect
- Why would you use a pendulum?
- How to use a pendulum
- When to use a pendulum
- How does the pendulum work?
- Other ideomotor signals

The Principles of Induction
- Understanding and purpose
- Comfortable position
- Hypnotic voice
- Utilisation
- Embedded commands and suggestions

- Deepening trance
- Recognising trance
- Awareness of client

The Induction Process
- Relaxation Induction

Designing Therapy
- Using stories and symbols
- Post-hypnotic suggestions
- Coming out of trance

Outcomes and Evaluation
- Important to monitor progress
- If they have not got the results, need to identify why not
- If they have got results, how else can you help

Taking Care with Hypnosis
- Don't over-claim or over-promise
- Stick to your field of competence
- Avoid clients with traumatic issues
- Be careful when dealing with medical issues
- Consider recording sessions

Self Hypnosis
- All hypnosis is self hypnosis
- Talking yourself into trance

Section 3: Hypnosis Scripts
3.1: Alternative Induction Scripts

These scripts are alternatives to the general induction script we included in Chapter 2.6.

You may find different scripts suit your personal style or could be more appropriate for different clients.

Elevator Induction
This script could be used on its own as along with another to deepen the relaxation.

>*Imagine yourself at the top of a tall building, maybe 20 or 30 stories high.*
>
>*See yourself getting into the lift on the very top floor. Look for the buttons and then get ready to press the button for the first floor.*
>
>*You'll watch those numbers above the lift door as you descend. With each number you see, you will notice yourself going deeper and deeper.*
>
>*By the time you reach the ground floor, you will be deeply relaxed. You'll be*

ready to listen to me and follow the powerful and positive suggestions I make about how to improve your life.

So press that button and start going down to the ground floor now...

Notice those numbers change as you go down. 19, 18, 17, 16, 15 ...with each floor you are getting more and more relaxed, concentrating just on where you are at this moment.

Deeply relaxed...

14, 13, 12... more and more relaxed as you go deeper and deeper.

Feeling calm, relaxed and comfortable...

11, 10, 9... so relaxed. Down, down, more and more

8, 7, 6... now feeling so relaxed. Feeling more deeply relaxed with each number.

5, 4, 3... you are feeling asleep, relaxed and at ease

2 even deeper

1 and so asleep as you reach the ground totally relaxed.

Elman Induction

This induction is one based on the principles from Dave Elman. His view was that hypnosis had to be directive. You had to tell the client exactly what to do.

With Elman inductions, it's important that the client follows your instructions exactly. If they do not follow you exactly, stay at that level until they do. If they anticipate your instruction, repeat the step so that they **follow** it.

Take a long deep breath and close your eyes. (You can start by holding your hand above their eyes and then moving it down to their chin as you say this.)

Now relax those muscles around the eyes to the point that they won't work... and pretend that you can't open them even though you know full well that you can. As long as you hold on to this level of relaxation, you can pretend that they just won't work.

When you're sure that they're so relaxed

111

*that they just won't work, continue to pretend that they won't work and test them to make sure that **they won't work**. Test them hard, that's right!*

Now let that feeling of relaxation go all the way down to your toes.

Now open your eyes. Really relax. Close your eyes again. That's it!

The next time you do this, you'll be able to relax even more than you have relaxed already.

Open your eyes. Close your eyes. Double the relaxation.

Open your eyes. Close your eyes. Double the relaxation.

Now I'm going to lift your hand and drop it. I want it to be as limp as a rag.

If you have followed my instructions, that relaxation will have gone down to your toes.

And when I lift your hand, it will just plop down. Let it fall. Totally relaxed!

That's right! (Lift their hand at this point and then let it fall.)

Now, physically, you have all the relaxation you need.

We want your mind to be as relaxed as your body is. So I want you to start counting down from 100 when I tell you to.

Each time you say a number, double your mental relaxation.

With each number you say, let your mind become twice as relaxed.

By the time you get down to 98, you'll be so relaxed the numbers won't be there.

Start form 100 and watch them disappear by the time you get to 98.

Double your relaxation and watch them start fading.

Now watch them disappear. Now they'll be gone. Isn't that a nice feeling?

Are they all gone? Let them disappear. Are they all gone? That's right.

3.2: Stop Smoking Script

In this section, we include some suggested scripts you can use after you have completed the induction and the client is in trance.

The first is for someone giving up smoking.

There are huge numbers of people who say they want to give up smoking but haven't yet found a way to kick the habit.

Many of these people would be interested in the option of self-hypnosis as a way to give up more easily. But the best prospects are those who really want to give up – rather than saying they want to give up or having been told they should.

For this group, you want to spend a lot of time in the interview talking about the reasons they want to give up. Find out how they think their life will be better when they do give up. You can then use this information to feedback to them in the suggestions.

Therefore you'd want to tailor this script based on what the person says are their reasons.

From your interview, identify the top five

reasons your client has given for wanting to give up smoking. (Ask them to confirm that these are the top 5.)

In addition to planning what you say, bear in mind that smoking is a habit and you need to help them plan strategies to assist the process. This could include finding something to chew or to hold in their hand as a replacement for the cigarette.

You would use the following script after you have gone through the appropriate induction and deepening and you have them in the trance you want.

> *I want you to imagine it is one year from today.*
>
> *You have now been a non-smoker for one year. You feel great due to the fresh air you can now breathe and you love how you feel physically, mentally, and emotionally.*
>
> *You now enjoy going out for a drink with your friends, feeling relaxed and comfortable without feeling any desire for a cigarette.*

You are proud that you were able to get rid of this habit and start enjoying life to the full again.

You see yourself at a party and laugh as someone offers you a cigarette. 'Why would anyone want one of those"', you ask.

[Make use of the client's list here to include more benefits they'll enjoy and use as many of the senses as possible in your descriptions.]

You love the smell of flowers as you walk in the clear country air in a way you were never able to enjoy before.

You love the taste of a cup of coffee or a glass of wine. A much more pleasant and enjoyable taste than you'd ever realised.

You have used your power of choice to choose to enjoy these experiences.

You know that you have the power to choose one deep breath any time you feel that old urge to light up.

One deep breath becomes a satisfying replacement for that old bad habit.

The physical replacement for yesterday's breath of smoke is one deep breath of air.

The mental replacement for yesterday's urge is your new friend, freedom to focus your mind or imagination on whatever you choose, because you love your power of choice.

You love your power of choice. And like a muscle that's used, it becomes stronger with use.

Imagine using that power of choice right now.

Imagine a situation that used to trigger the urge to a light up.

Now take a deep breath and relax... Choose something fun, enjoyable, beautiful, or pleasant to imagine.

Like a muscle, your power of choice becomes stronger with use.

Every time you take that deep breath, it becomes easier and easier to choose the deep breath instead of the old slave master.

You are a non smoker now, because the benefits are so satisfying and rewarding.

You love your power of choice!

Now once again imagine another event that would have triggered the urge to light up before.

As you do, take a deep breath and relax. Now imagine something fun, enjoyable, beautiful or pleasant.

You are already practicing your ability to use your new power freedom to be a non smoker.

Yesterday's urges are simply forgotten... fading away into the mists of time, vanishing into the fog of forgetfulness, replaced with your new friend, freedom.

You are free to focus your mind, thoughts or actions on whatever you choose – whether at work or play, at home or away from home, alone or with others.

You love your power of choice, and it was your choice to become a non smoker.

Now it is your choice to put your mind to whatever you choose.

Your decision is bringing you the benefits you have chosen...

[Restate some of the client's desired benefits they'll enjoy. Help them establish a strong positive connection with enjoying the benefits]

Now imagine your benefits so strongly that you feel as though you already enjoy success.

You love your power of choice and every day it becomes easier and easier for you automatically to take that deep breath at times you used to light up.

You feel more and more like a non smoker with each passing day, as the deep breath becomes a totally satisfying replacement for yesterday's unhealthy urge.

Simply decide that you are now a non smoker because you chose to be, and you love your power of choice.

Imagine your success so powerfully that all of these ideas and suggestions simply go deeper and deeper into your mind, becoming a part of you simply because you choose them.

Then when you next hear my voice, it will be almost time to come back.

Then after a short silence, awaken the client slowly.

3.3: Weight Loss Script

Another powerful use of hypnosis is to help people achieve their desired weight.

Again, the interview process is important in developing the right script for the individual. If they want to lose weight, you need to establish their reasons for being overweight.

There is no point in planting suggestions about going to the gym if somebody is eating the wrong food.

As with any type of hypnosis, you need to confine your comments to changing habits and working on emotions. It's important to establish early on if the client has any kind of medical problem or serious psychological issue that could be inflaming the issue.

Take care to refer any serious medical or psychological issues to an appropriately qualified professional.

Nevertheless there are many ways you can help someone develop the right way of thinking and self-belief to lose weight.

Today you can make a choice about the rest of your life.

You can make a decision to leave things the way they have been for several years.

Or you can choose to make a change.

You can choose a lifestyle of health and greater happiness.

You can choose to look great and feel great. You can choose to have the lifestyle you want.

I'm going to count to 3 and when I reach 3, I want you to go forward one year from today.

1, 2 and 3

Now look back on the past year of your life – the new life you enjoyed after that change you made one year ago today.

Notice your body and how slim you feel. Notice how healthy you feel because you have been eating well.

Think of preparing to go out for dinner with your partner and slipping into that beautiful new outfit.

Enjoy the moment as you admire yourself in the mirror.

Think about being able to go out and enjoy wonderful food and feeling good about it.

Congratulate yourself for that change you made in your life when you decided to eat well and go to the gym regularly.

You are proud that you were able to change your lifestyle and start enjoying life to the full again.

[Make use of the client's list here to include more benefits they'll enjoy and use as many of the senses as possible in your descriptions.]

You love the smell of that beautiful dinner.

You love the taste of a small glass of champagne.

123

You used your power of choice to choose to enjoy these experiences.

You know that you have the power to say no to that snack food you used to nibble on.

You know that you have the power to say yes to going to the gym when you used to find an excuse.

I'm now going to count back to 1 and I want you to come back to today.

3, 2 and 1

Now in your mind decide to make the choice that will give you that picture one year from today

You love your power of choice. And like a muscle that's used, it becomes stronger with use.

Imagine using that power of choice right now.

Imagine a situation that used to trigger

the urge to eat junk food.

Now take a deep breath and relax...
Choose something fun, enjoyable,
beautiful, or pleasant to imagine.

Remember that feeling of relaxation
every time you take a deep breath.

Every time you take that deep breath in
future, it will become easier and easier to
choose the healthy option.

When you face options that used to be
tempting, learn to take that deep breath
and make the healthy choice.

You eat healthily now, because the
benefits are so satisfying and rewarding.

You love your power of choice!

Now imagine an event that in the past
would have triggered an excuse to skip
the gym.

As you do, take a deep breath and relax.
Now imagine something fun, enjoyable,
beautiful or pleasant.

Make the choice to go to the gym and enjoy it.

You are already practicing your ability to use your new power freedom to live healthily.

Yesterday's urges are simply forgotten... fading away into the mists of time, vanishing into the fog of forgetfulness, replaced with your new friend, choice.

You love your power of choice, and it was your choice to become a slim person.

It was your choice to start eating healthily and to go to the gym regularly.

Now it is your choice to put your mind to whatever you choose.

Your decision is bringing you the benefits you have chosen...

[Restate some of the client's desired benefits they'll enjoy. Help them establish a strong positive connection with enjoying the benefits]

Now imagine your benefits so strongly that you feel as though you already enjoy success.

You love your power of choice and every day it becomes easier and easier for you to say no to junk food and say yes to going to the gym.

You enjoy your healthy living more and more with each passing day, as eating healthily and going to the gym becomes a totally satisfying replacement for yesterday's unhealthy urge.

Simply decide that you are now a healthy eater because you chose to be, and you love your power of choice.

Simply decide that you enjoy going to the gym because you choose to, and you love your power of choice.

You choose to be healthy.

Imagine your success so powerfully that all of these ideas and suggestions simply go deeper and deeper into your mind, becoming a part of you simply because you choose them.

Then when you next hear my voice, it will be almost time to come back.

Then after a short silence, awaken the client slowly.

3.4: Skills Improvement Script

Hypnosis is a very powerful way to help people develop and make the most of their skills.

Often what separates good performers in any field – whether it is sport or business – is the mindset with which they approach what they are doing.

The golfer who stays focused on the hole will have more chance of sinking the putt than one who is worried about missing.

In business, the person who is a good public speaker – but is held back by nerves – is at a disadvantage compared with others who have less skill but more confidence.

Hypnosis can therefore help individuals develop and improve the skills they need to succeed in their chosen field.

This example scripts covers someone improving their putting skills but it can easily be applied for any performance improvement.

Today you have become a significantly better golfer.

Now you can putt like a superstar.

Every time you walk onto a putting green, you feel calm, confident and focused, you know you are going to hole most of your putts.

In a moment, I'm going to ask you to picture yourself next time you are on the putting green and ready to take a putt that used to be challenging for you.

Forget all about the way you used to feel when taking that sort of putt.

That's all in the past. That's nothing to do with who you are now.

Be ready to change the way you putt.

I'm going to count to 3 and when I reach 3, I want you to go in your imagination onto the putting green as you get ready to take an important putt.

I want you to take into that moment the same relaxation that you have now. You feel totally calm, confident and focused.

1, 2 and 3

Notice how different you feel compared to before. You are relaxed, calm and confident.

You know you have the skills to do this. You just need to prepare yourself properly.

So take time to look at what needs to be done. Imagine what Tiger Woods or another great golfer would do in this situation.

You can hole this putt too.

You are calm and confident as you check out what needs to be done. You are focused on the hole.

Then you lean over the ball and look at it from there.

In your mind's eye, see yourself putting that ball into the hole.

Hear the applause of others as it drops

into the hole.

Run that movie through your mind several times – noticing what you needed to do to putt the ball into the hole.

Now take a step back and take a deep breath,

As you take that deep breath, feel that sense of deep relaxation, complete confidence and total focus.

Now go back to your putter and complete the job. Putt the ball into the hole. That's right.

This time you really enjoy the applause of the others as you sink that putt. They are impressed. You are now so much better than you were before.

I'm now going to count back to 1 and I want you to come back to today in your mind but staying here in deep relaxation.

3, 2 and 1

Today you changed the way you play golf forever.

From now on, every time you step on a putting green, you will immediately have that feeling of calmness, confidence and focus.

Every time you pick up your putter, you will know you are going to putt like a pro.

Every time you take that deep breath when you get ready to take the shot, you will feel that deep sense of relaxation that you enjoy now.

Now and every time you putt in the future, you will have calm confidence in your ability.

Enjoy this moment of pleasure about your new abilities.

Congratulate yourself for this change you have made in your life.

[Make use of any information the client has given you about the benefits they'll enjoy when they have made this change and use as many of the senses as possible in your descriptions.]

Then when you next hear my voice, it will be almost time to come back.

Then after a short silence, awaken the client slowly.

3.5: Additional Script Ideas

The following bullet points suggest key points to consider when creating hypnosis plans for some other issues.

Relaxation

- Stress can cause unhappiness, ill-health, reduced work effectiveness and relationship problems

- People often resort to medication to control it or choose alternative releases such as alcohol

- Being able to find an effective way to control or reduce stress is therefore very powerful

- Hypnosis can heighten the body's natural ability to relax, leading to effects such as deeper breathing, better blood flow and normalized metabolism

- Learning to relax has a trigger effect that improves other areas of the operation of the mind and body

- Hypnosis has a natural effect of making people relax

- It can also be used to plant suggestions about being able to relax in specific situations

Pain control

- Pain is usually a warning from the body to pay attention to something so in that sense pain is useful

- The objective is therefore not to get rid of pain completely

- But sometimes pain continues after we have started to deal with a problem – for example pain after an operation or discomfort during an illness

- In those circumstances it is good to be able to control pain

- Sometimes pain is an indication of something psychological such as stress so it is possible not only to deal with the pain but to address the cause of it as well

- Hypnosis can be very effective at dealing with this type of pain

- With proper strategies, hypnosis can also be used in medical and dental surgery procedures instead of anaesthetic

- Hypnosis can also be used to manage the effect of chronic pain such as joint or muscle pain

Self confidence

- Lack of self confidence is an issue that holds many people back from achieving their full potential

- The problem is that it's not an illness that people can recognise the symptoms of and decide to take action on

- People develop different levels of self confidence depending on their background and environment

- While for some people, it's a major issue, for others its just something that limits them without them feeling they need to act

- However self confidence is purely in the mind and therefore it's possible to change anyone's level of self-confidence

- You can help people construct a different picture of themselves and their abilities to change the results they achieve

- Hypnosis is a great way of helping people build up a different picture of themselves with a very powerful outcome

Overcoming fears

- Many people suffer from fears, anxiety and phobias that have a major impact on their lives

- The effects can be specific to particular events – such as a racing heart when faced with public speaking

- They can also be generalised to a feeling of irritability or sleep difficulties that apply over an extended period

- These problems can have a major effect on people's lives ranging from preventing

them doing things they want to do to
serious long-term health problems

- Some people choose to live with these
  problems because they don't see any way
  out

- But there are often significant benefits to
  the person in addressing the problem

- Hypnosis can be used to help the person
  take control of the issue and deal with
  the symptoms

- It can also address the underlying issue
  so that the problem will disappear
  completely

Thinking about money

- Many people are not making the money
  they want to in their lives

- The reason for this is often unconscious
  attitudes they have developed in the past,
  such as "All people with money are bad"
  or "I'll never have much money"

- While thinking alone is not going to make

anyone rich, the wrong type of thinking can easily prevent you from being successful

- Therefore being able to change someone's negative attitudes about money into positive ones can have a powerful effect on their lives

- Hypnosis can be used to change these attitudes

- It can also be used to help people create clear goals for themselves and a clear mental picture of the success they want

- By helping people change their thinking about money, you can help them earn more

INDEX

141

HypnosisPractitioner

Hypnosis has long caught the imagination of people throughout history.

Learn to tap into this powerhouse of a resource that resides inside you, and in so doing, transforming your understanding of self and others.

- *Forms and levels of Trance*
- *Formal and Informal hypnosis*
- *The ethics of hypnosis and why this is important*
- *How to use scripts and how to create your own scripts*
- *Master of the art of suggestions*
- *How to utilise each of the major areas of hypnosis*
- *How to utilise hypnotic interview*
- *Recognising the different levels of trance*
- *Creating trance using the power of your voice*
- *Deepening trance techniques*
- *How to utilize hypnosis phenomena*

The manual covers the background information that is needed to fully understand how hypnosis works and where it can be utilized. All of this backed up with full multi media.

"A benchmark for how training and learning should be delivered/facilitated, professional, ethical and damn good fun Thanks"
Andrew Drummond

Hypnosis Master Practitioner

When you are ready to take your Hypnosis skills to the next level then the Hypnosis Master Practitioner is for you.

You will explore:
- Stopping Smoking techniques
- Wight Loss techniques
- Habit control
- Limiting beliefs

Going beyond scripts and understanding human behaviour you will be able to tailor your skills to the individual.

You will also explore different types of hypnosis including the work of Dave Elman.

Regression techniques for:
- Past lives
- Finding lost items
- Finding memories
- Enhancing learning skills

With the live training you will also have access to our online members area which has a growing range of workbooks, videos, audio and online courses. All been designed to for life long learning. We also offer you the chance to retake the live training as many times as you wish.

NLP Practitioner

*To complement your hypnosis training we
recommend you take our NLP Practitioner training.*

This program will certify you as a Practitioner of Neuro-Linguistic Programming. NLP is a methodology for modelling excellence in human behaviour.

Initially created in the 1970's by Richard Bandler and John Grinder, NLP has consistently explored and duplicated the behavioural processes of individuals who effectively create results in their lives.

The discoveries made from the methodology of NLP have led to techniques that are used in therapy, business, health and education. NLP is a very practical approach to human behaviour. It is primarily focused on how to operate your own mind and body to create what you want in life. In this certificated course, you will be presented with skills that you can use in your own life for generating successful results, and tools for helping others attain their goals, dreams and aspirations.

You will learn a set of skills that can be the foundation for all the goals in your life. We will take you to the roots of understanding and behaviour. Before NLP we had explanations as to why we act in certain ways. Since NLP we have the understanding of how we act in those ways. Throughout this training you will uncover and work with the processes that precede behaviour. You will learn the very fabric of thought and action. It is often said that NLP has made the greatest contribution to the behavioural sciences in the last 30 years. Become a Certified Practitioner of NLP and become your very best!

You will own the NLP language and be able to use it in your everyday life:
• *Using conversational hypnosis*
• *Using natural conversation to facilitate change in others*
• *Learn to embed idea's, learning's and suggestions in peoples' minds*
• *Learn to be precise with your questioning skills*
• *Able to track beliefs through language*
• *Use language to influence and inspire others*

Visit www.free-nlp.co.uk to find out more or email john@free-nlp.co.uk

Your notes: